A Children's Book On Bishop Richard Allen

A Nonviolent Journey

Written by: Argrow "Kit" Evans-Ford

Illustrated by: Rev. Dionne Nicole Carter

Testimonies of Hope Press

Testimonies of Hope

Author's Note

A few years ago I was looking through my Grandma Argrow's Bible and a brochure of Bishop Richard Allen fell out. It talked about his life and legacy. I thought, "What was it about Bishop Richard Allen that caused my grandmother to hold him as an inspiring example?" She was a local deacon in the African Methodist Episcopal Church (AMEC) and had such a compassionate heart. She taught me how to love God and others.

I researched and saw that his life had modeled something so powerful for my grandmother. In turn she had modeled these same qualities for our family: *freedom, faith, family, education, nonviolence, courage, and love.* I thought it necessary for me to write, *A Children's Book On Bishop Richard Allen: A Nonviolent Journey*, so all children can understand the life and legacy of such an important person in the AME Church and our history.

I pray this story of hope inspires you!

-Argrow "Kit" Evans-Ford

Word Scholar!

Watch out; these words are very important.

Freedom

Faith

Family

Education

Nonviolence

Courage

Love

Text copyright © 2014 by Argrow Kitnequa Evans-Ford.
Illustrations copyright © 2014 by
Argrow Kitnequa Evans-Ford. All rights reserved.
Published by Testimonies of Hope Press
PO Box 3951, Rock Island, IL 61204
To order individual copies or bulk copies,
visit: www.achildrensbookonrichardallen.com

Library of Congress Cataloging-in Publication Data
ISBN- 13: 978-0-692-20896-0
ISBN- 10: 0-692-20896-8

Book Design: Lauryn Van Fleet Crowley
Editor: Argrow "Kit" Evans-Ford

For **The Reverend Argrow Margaret Warren**

Grandma

Bobbi: Hi Grandma Argrow!

Grandma Argrow: Praise the Lord, baby! What are you up to little Bobbi?

Bobbi: I'm just playing around, Grandma Argrow! I found your Bible and this paper fell out. Who is this man, Grandma?

Grandma Argrow: Sweetheart, this is a brochure of the Bishop Richard Allen. He was a great, courageous man, who loved his family, and founded our denomination, the African Methodist Episcopal Church!

Bobbi: Oh, wow! That's a big deal. He sounds cool.

Grandma Argrow: Ha ha. Yes, sweetheart, he is cool! Let's sit down and I will tell you a story about him.

Grandma Argrow:
Grab your tomato sandwich and apple juice.
You can eat it while I tell you the story. I know
you are hungry!

Bobbi:
You know me well, Grandma!

Grandma Argrow:
Here we go, sweetheart!

A long time ago, in the year 1760, a boy named Richard was born in the colony of Philadelphia. He was an African American slave who dreamed of becoming a free man.

"I was born in the year 1760, on February 14th, a slave to Benjamin Chew, of Philadelphia."

– Bishop Richard Allen

When Richard was 7 years old, he and his family were sold to Farmer Stokley in Delaware. Richard, his parents, and siblings worked long backbreaking hours as field hands for Stokley.

10 years later, when Richard was 17 years old, his mother and three siblings were taken away and sold. Richard never saw them again! This made Richard very sad, because he adored his family.

His family was torn apart by slavery, which deeply hurt his mother's heart. But, he knew she was close to God and strong!

"My mother sought the Lord and found favor with him."

– Bishop Richard Allen

Soon after his family was sold, Richard's slave master told him that he could buy his freedom for $2,000.

Richard stayed in the fields working on the slave plantation day and night to earn money. He was determined to become free!

"I had it often impressed upon my mind that I should one day enjoy my freedom; for slavery is a bitter pill."

-Bishop Richard Allen

When Richard was a teenager, he attended the Methodist Society meetings. White preachers in the Methodist Society allowed slaves and free African American people to attend these religious meetings.

Soon after his church visits began, Richard realized he wanted to become a preacher. He loved God with all of his heart!

"I cried unto God who delighted to hear my prayers, and all of the sudden my chains flew off, and glory to God, I cried. My soul was filled."

-Bishop Richard Allen

Most slaves never got to hold a book or a pen in their hands. Slave masters did not want their slaves to be educated and know there was a world outside of slavery.

However, Richard taught himself how to read and write. Education was very important to him. He was smart and courageous!

In the year, 1783, at the age of 23, Richard bought his freedom from slavery. He worked really hard for the $2,000!

Richard had an older brother on the same slave plantation who he loved dearly. He could not bear to leave him so they saved enough money to purchase both of their freedom from slavery.

"A door was opened up unexpectedly for me to buy my time and enjoy my liberty."

-Bishop Richard Allen

Although, Richard was now a free man, he still worked hard, cutting wood with blistered hands to earn bread for food. Richard's heart was still devoted to serving God.

"While my hands were employed to earn my bread, my heart was devoted to my dear Redeemer. Sometimes I would awake from my sleep preaching and praying."

-Bishop Richard Allen

On Sept 3, 1783, Richard left Delaware and walked from state to state preaching the gospel. It took courage and faith for him to travel those long distances by foot. He preached in Delaware, New Jersey, Maryland, and Pennsylvania.

"After leaving Wilmington, I went into New Jersey, and there traveled and strove to preach the Gospel until the spring of 1784. I walked until my feet became so sore and blistered, that I scarcely could bear them to the ground."

-Bishop Richard Allen

"Methodist"

Richard started to preach in the Methodist Episcopal Church denomination, where Black and White people went to church together. Preachers were also Black and White.

The founder of Methodism, John Wesley, was against slavery. This was the way Richard wanted his church to be.

"I was confident that there was no religious denomination [that] would suit the capacity of the colored people as well as the Methodist. The reason that the Methodist is so successful in the awakening and conversion of the colored people, the plain doctrine and having a good discipline."

-Bishop Richard Allen

St. George's Methodist Episcopal

In 1786, Richard became a preacher at St. George Methodist Episcopal Church in Philadelphia. He preached with boldness at the 5:00 am services. He also began to help the Black community in Philadelphia.

He saw that in the Declaration of Independence all people were to be "free and equal." In reality, whites created laws that made it much harder for Blacks to own land or get an education.

"I strove to preach as well as I could, but it was a great cross to me; but the Lord was with me. I soon saw a large field open in seeking and instructing my African brethren, who had been a long forgotten people."

-Bishop Richard Allen

White preachers at St. George got upset about Reverend Allen's work. But he did not stop. He found another way to help African American people. He worked around the laws to assist other Black Americans that had also managed to escape slavery. Like him, they were free, but still worked hard and had very little money.

In 1787, Richard cofounded the Free African Society to provide medical care, better education for children, help with using money wisely, and other services his community needed.

These really great programs were met with conflict because of racism. Some respected people of color within Philadelphia and also White Elders within the Methodist Episcopal Church rejected the programs.

"I established prayer meetings; I raised a society in 1786 of forty-two members. I saw the necessity of erecting a place of worship for the colored people. The elder soon forbid us holding any such meetings. They were considered a nuisance."

-Bishop Richard Allen

The number of Black people attending St. George Methodist Episcopal Church increased greatly. Blacks were soon moved from their usual seat area to seats around the wall and in the balcony, separating them from White church attendees. White people were seen as superior to Blacks.

Richard and his minister friends, Absalom Jones and William White, were used to sitting at the front on the sanctuary, but they had to move because of the color of their skin.

"When the colored people began to get numerous in attending the church, they moved us from the seats we usually sat on, and placed us around the wall."

-Bishop Richard Allen

In November of 1787, Richard, Absalom, and William attended service. Without thinking they went to their usual seats on the bottom floor. It was prayer time, so they went to pray. They were on their knees praying when a trustee of the church came and told them they could not pray in the front of the church because they were Black.

Absalom asked the trustee to wait for them to finish their prayers, but the trustee attempted to pull them off of their knees away from the altar. Before they could drag them out of the church, all three men finished their prayer.

The remaining Black church members walked out of the church with Richard, Absalom, and William. Though the trustees were very violent, Black church members were nonviolent and did not meet violence with violence. They walked out together peacefully standing against racism and injustice. This was one of the first documented nonviolent demonstrations by African Americans.

"We had not been long upon our knees before I heard considerable scuffling and low talking. I raised my head up and saw one of the trustees, H-- M--, having hold of the Rev. Absalom Jones, pulling him up off of his knees, and saying, 'You must get up--you must not kneel here.' Mr. Jones replied, 'wait until prayer is over.' Mr. H-- M-- said 'no, you must get up now, or I will call for aid and I force you away.' Mr. Jones said, 'wait until prayer is over, and I will get up and trouble you no more.' With that he beckoned to one of the other trustees, Mr. L-- S-- to come to his assistance. He came, and went to William White to pull him up. By this time prayer was over, and we all went out of the church in a body, and they were no more plagued with us in the church."

-Bishop Richard Allen

Richard wanted to start a church where Black people would be accepted and treated as equal, where they would feel comfortable and safe worshiping and praying.

Richard discovered an old blacksmith shop and bought it for $30. He had it repaired to start his first church. Richard eventually hauled the shop with a team of horses and moved the church to 6th and Lombard Street in Philadelphia.

"We bore much persecution from many of the Methodist connection; but we have reason to be thankful to Almighty God, who was our deliverer. We believed if we put our trust in the Lord, he would stand by us."

-Bishop Richard Allen

On July 29, 1794, Bethel African Methodist Episcopal Church was dedicated and Richard Allen became the first pastor. Bethel means "House of God." Bethel AME became a place of hope and liberation for African Americans.

After much struggle between Blacks and Whites within the Methodist Episcopal Church, the African Methodist Episcopal Church was founded in 1816. Black people were grateful to God to now have a religious community where they could learn, worship, and live freely.

"Bethel surrounded by her foes,
But not yet in despair,
Christ heard her supplicating cries;
The God of Bethel heard."

-Bishop Richard Allen

Family

Richard served as a pastor, husband, and father. He also worked as a shoemaker to support his family financially. Though Richard was a busy man, he still made time for his family. Allen was first married to Flora Allen, a former slave. However, she died in March of 1801. Later he met and married Sarah Allen in August of 1801. She was also a former slave, who was now free.

Sarah served with Richard within the AME Church. She became the church's first female missionary and also aided in assisting runaway slaves who were seeking freedom through the Underground Railroad. She was a strong woman and Richard respected his wife.

Sarah and Richard had six children together. Their names were Richard Jr., Sara, Peter, James, Ann, and John.

Richard, who eventually became Bishop Richard Allen at the age of 56, was a courageous leader during difficult times.

The African Methodist Episcopal Church was the first independent Black denomination. And that was only the beginning of the AME tradition. Today the African Methodist Episcopal Church is located in thirty-nine countries, five continents, and continues to grow!

Bishop Richard Allen's legacy of equality, love, and justice is still with us today. He even embraced nonviolence during a time when he and other Black Americans were threatened with violence. When you have a tough day, remember, Bishop Richard Allen's actions.

Bishop Richard Allen died on March 26, 1831 at the age of 71.   His body was buried in a tomb at the lower level of Mother Bethel AME Church in Philadelphia. Though he is no longer alive, the story of his life lives on for generations to come!

"My labor was much blessed."

-Bishop Richard Allen

Grandma Argrow: Well sweetie, that's the life and legacy of Bishop Richard Allen.

Bobbi: What a story Grandma Argrow! I can see why you had his brochure in your Bible all of these years.

Grandma Argrow: Yes, sweetheart. When I am having a hard time in life, sometimes I think about the strength, courage, and faith of Bishop Richard Allen. He went from slavery to freedom to Bishop. I think about how he loved the church and his family. I also think about how he lived a nonviolent journey.

Bobbi: Grandma, what does nonviolence mean?

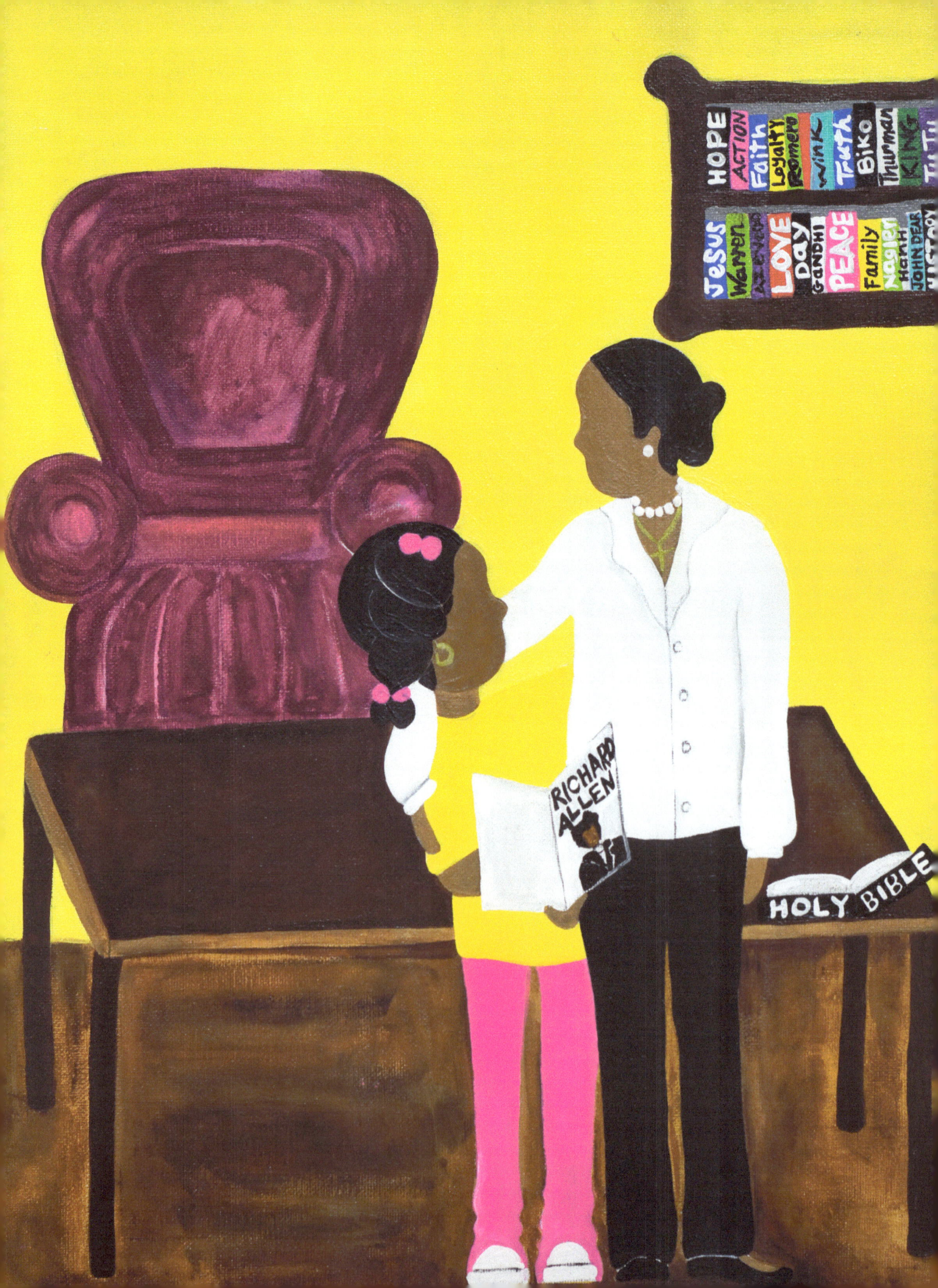

Grandma Argrow: Sweetie, you remember in the story when Bishop Richard Allen and his friends were pulled off of their knees for praying at the front of the church because they were African American? Instead of using their power to hit the other person, they turned the other cheek and walked away peacefully. It takes courage to be peaceful when someone tries to hurt you.

Bishop Allen and his friends were courageous. They stood up against injustice by organizing and helping their community, the African American community. They started their own church, advocated for education for their children, and found resources that provided medical care for their families. Bishop Allen used his energy to help people, instead of hurt people.

Bobbi: So, Grandma, we help people instead of hurt people?

Grandma Argrow: Yes, my child. Regardless of skin color, gender, how much money a person makes, or any difference. We have to remember this important life lesson: Help people instead of hurt people!

Bobbi: I love you Grandma! That was a great story and that was also a great tomato sandwich! I can't wait to share this story at church and school with my friends.

Bishop Allen is a lot like you Grandma. You are courageous, strong, and help people. You love God and your family too Grandma!

Grandma Argrow: Thank you, baby! That means a lot. I'm glad you liked the story. Now come on over here and give your Grandma some sugar!

 Bobbi: Grandma, not the kisses! I love you.

Grandma Argrow: I love you too baby!

Timeline

Learning about Bishop Richard Allen's life, we can see that everything he did was a service to God and to others.

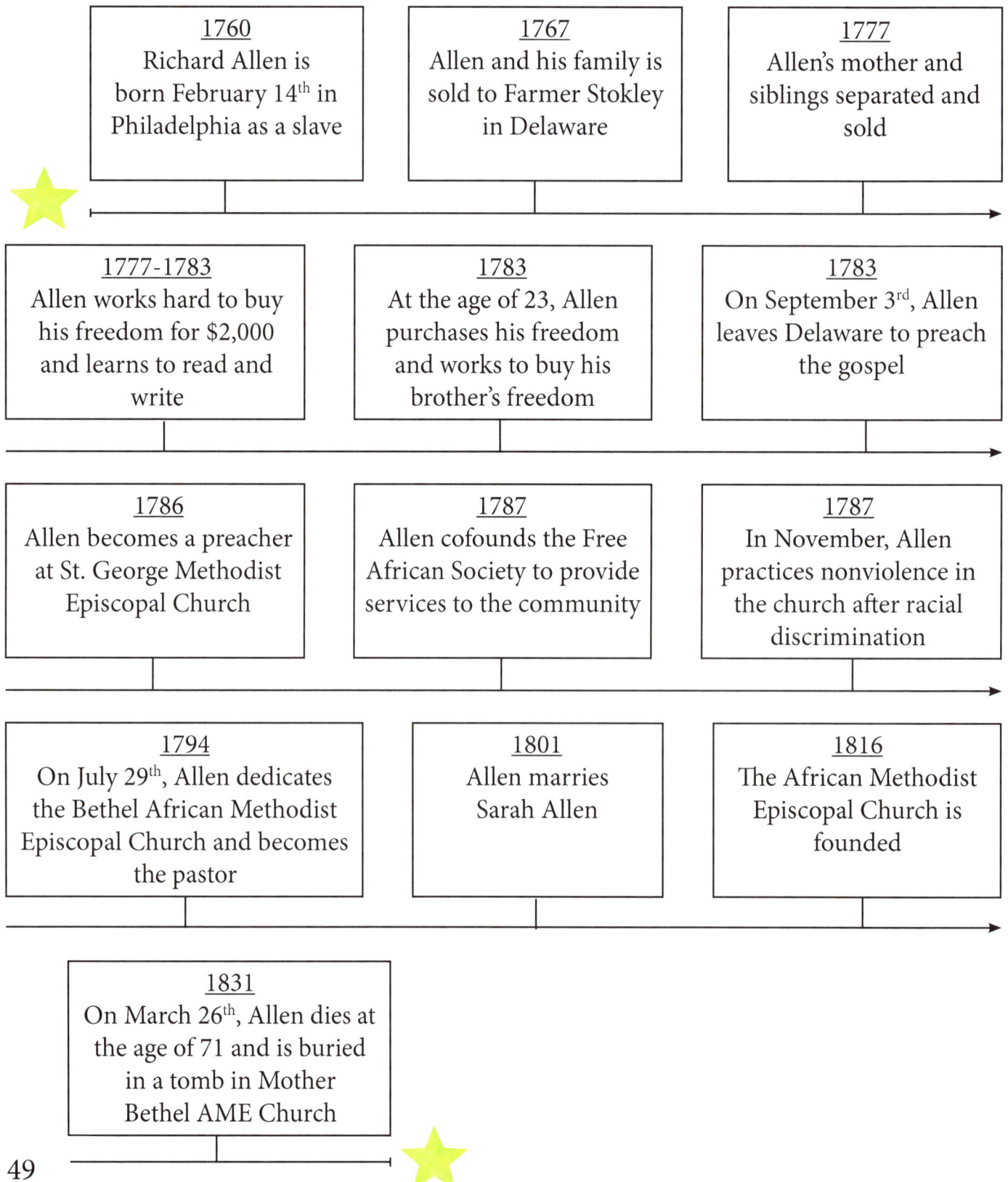

1760 Richard Allen is born February 14th in Philadelphia as a slave	**1767** Allen and his family is sold to Farmer Stokley in Delaware	**1777** Allen's mother and siblings separated and sold

1777-1783 Allen works hard to buy his freedom for $2,000 and learns to read and write	**1783** At the age of 23, Allen purchases his freedom and works to buy his brother's freedom	**1783** On September 3rd, Allen leaves Delaware to preach the gospel

1786 Allen becomes a preacher at St. George Methodist Episcopal Church	**1787** Allen cofounds the Free African Society to provide services to the community	**1787** In November, Allen practices nonviolence in the church after racial discrimination

1794 On July 29th, Allen dedicates the Bethel African Methodist Episcopal Church and becomes the pastor	**1801** Allen marries Sarah Allen	**1816** The African Methodist Episcopal Church is founded

1831 On March 26th, Allen dies at the age of 71 and is buried in a tomb in Mother Bethel AME Church

Additional Resources

A Children's Book On Bishop Richard Allen: A Nonviolent Journey (Curriculum)

This curriculum is to be used with, *A Children's Book On Bishop Richard Allen: A Nonviolent Journey*, and highlights some of the ways that teachers and parents can extend learning for students. The activities include many subject areas. Language arts topics include: *Reading, Writing, Speaking, and Listening.* Social Studies topics include: *Genealogy, Geography, and History.* There are also lessons on *Anti-Bullying, Art, and Mathematics.* We give you many angles to look at and learn from Bishop Richard Allen's life. This curriculum is full of helpful content, creativity, and insightful insight for you and your students.

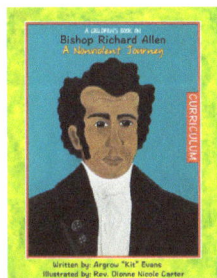

A Children's Book on Bishop Richard Allen: A Nonviolent Journey (Art Exhibit Tour)

Would you like see a live art exhibit on Bishop Richard Allen? Each illustration within *A Children's Book on Bishop Richard Allen: A Nonviolent Journey* is a live 16 x 20 acrylic painting. The collection of 20 beautiful, colorful, and historical paintings take you on a visual journey of the life and legacy of Bishop Richard Allen. The vibrant paintings model the character traits that Bishop Richard Allen exemplifies for children today: *Freedom, Faith, Family, Education, Nonviolence, Courage, and Love.* Bring this amazing art exhibit to your church, school, or community organization today!

Would you like to bring Author, Argrow "Kit" Evans-Ford, to your church, school, community organization, or group? Speakers Requests, Workshops, and Teacher Trainings are available upon request.

Order your *A Children's Book On Bishop Richard Allen: A Nonviolent Journey* resources today by visiting:

www.achildrensbookonrichardallen.com

Bibliography

Allen, Richard. "Address to the Free Persons of Colour in the United States." Sermon, Free Persons of Colour Convention, Philadelphia, PA, September 20, 1830. http://faculty.sanjuancollege.edu/krobison/documents/Address-FreePersonsColour.htm (accessed August 7, 2014).

Allen, Richard. *The Life, Experience, and Gospel Labours of the Rt. Rev. Richard Allen: To Which is Annexed the Rise and Progress of the African Methodist Episcopal Church in the United States of America: Containing a Narrative of the Yellow Fever in the Year of Our Lord 1793: With an Address to the People of Colour in the United States.* New York: Abingdon Press, 1960.

Dickerson, Dennis C. *Religion, Race, and Region: Research Notes On A.M.E. Church History.* Nashville: AMEC Sunday School Union, 2005.

George, Carol V. R. *Richard Allen and the Emergence of Independent Black Churches 1760-1840.* New York: Oxford University Press, 1973.

Klots, Steve. *Richard Allen: Religious Leader and Social Activist.* New York: Chelsea House Publishers, 1991.

Mother Bethel AME Church. *Bishop Richard Allen: Apostle of Freedom (The Documentary).* DVD. Philadelphia: Mother Bethel AME Church, 2010.

Mwadilifu, Mwalimu I. *Richard Allen: The First Exemplar of African American Education.* New York: ECA Associates, 1985.

Newman, Richard S. *Freedom's Prophet: Bishop Richard Allen, the AME Church, and the Black Founding Fathers.* New York: New York University Press, 2008.

Wesley, Charles H. *Richard Allen: Apostle of Freedom.* Washington, DC: Associated Publishers, 1969.

About the Author

Argrow "Kit" Evans-Ford, MA, MAT, MDiv

Argrow "Kit" Evans-Ford is a woman who is passionate about nonviolence, God, and serving others. She has been a trainer, speaker, and activist for many years working relentlessly in nonviolence education, violence prevention, special education, and assisting people in healing from violence and abuse.

Born in Mebane, North Carolina, Kit grew up in the African Methodist Episcopal Church where many of her immediate family serve as ordained clergy. This includes her mother, the Rev. Dorothy Ann Warren and grandmother, the late Rev. Argrow Margaret Warren.

Kit holds graduate degrees in Teaching, Social Justice, Community Development as well as a Master of Divinity Degree. She is the founder of *Testimonies of Hope: The Intercultural Christian Devotional Community* at www.testimoniesofhope.org and *Overcoming the S.T.O.R.M: A Program For Women Healing From Sexual Violence*. Mrs. Evans-Ford is the author of *101 Testimonies of Hope: Life Stories To Encourage Your Faith In God* and *A Children's Book On Bishop Richard Allen: A Nonviolent Journey*.

Kit lives in Rock Island, Illinois with her husband, the Rev. Dwight L. Ford.

To learn more about Argrow "Kit" Evans-Ford, visit:

www.achildrensbookonrichardallen.com
www.kitevanslive.com

www.ingramcontent.com/pod-product-compliance
Lightning Source LLC
LaVergne TN
LVHW072107070426
835509LV00002B/50